D1531665

**The IBC Approach to
Understanding**

Who We Are
and How
We Relate

DR. LARRY CRABB

Dr. Tom Varney
Series Editor

NAVPRESS
BRINGING TRUTH TO LIFE
NavPress Publishing Group
P.O. Box 35001, Colorado Springs, Colorado 80935

The Navigators is an international Christian organization. Jesus Christ gave His followers the Great Commission to go and make disciples (Matthew 28:19). The aim of The Navigators is to help fulfill that commission by multiplying laborers for Christ in every nation.

NavPress is the publishing ministry of The Navigators. NavPress publications are tools to help Christians grow. Although publications alone cannot make disciples or change lives, they can help believers learn biblical discipleship, and apply what they learn to their lives and ministries.

ISBN 08910-96949

Fourth printing, 1994

Cover illustration: David Watts

The anecdotal illustrations in this book are composites of real situations, and any resemblance to people living or dead is coincidental.

All Scripture in this publication is from the *Holy Bible: New International Version* (NIV). Copyright © 1973, 1978, 1984, International Bible Society. Used by permission of Zondervan Bible Publishers.

Printed in the United States of America

FOR A FREE CATALOG OF
NAVPRESS BOOKS & BIBLE STUDIES,
CALL 1-800-366-7788 (USA)
or 1-416-499-4615 (CANADA)

CONTENTS

ва

INTRODUCTION
Understanding God's Design

ॐ

Life in Christ is all about relationships, with God, others, and ourselves. When we reduce Christianity to a series of steps for handling life better or a set of truths to believe or a list of things to do, we miss the whole point of the gospel.

God created (and then re-created) us to enjoy His kindness and loving generosity and, in the strength of that enjoyment, to reflect His character by giving ourselves unselfishly to each other. He meant for us to feel good about ourselves as people who understand that:

- Our *value* is rooted in His undeserved love.

- Our *purpose* is to give others a taste of God's goodness that points them to Christ.

- Our *hope* is being with Christ in a future day when every relationship will work exactly as planned.

But something has gone wrong. That's not the way we approach life. We've gotten off track in ways that have seriously changed how we handle relationships — beginning with how we relate to God.

LOOKING OUT FOR NUMBER ONE

We're not sure God is good enough to be fully trusted. Things that are important to us seem to be matters of indifference to Him. He permits helpless children to be abused, hardworking people to lose their jobs, faithful followers to die terrible deaths, families who sincerely try to do everything right to be ripped apart, and people who have sacrificed a lot for the Kingdom to struggle against perverted urges that create an awful sense of shame.

Trusting a God who tells us He loves us but then fails to protect us from the hard circumstances of life doesn't come easily.

And we're not at all persuaded that living our lives for the sake of others is a particularly smart thing to do. People, even the best ones, can be mean and petty. We've all been let down by someone we've trusted and hurt by someone we've tried to help. Sometimes the damage inflicted on us by others' mistreatment lingers for years and surfaces long after the harmful relationship has ended.

Perhaps it's a better idea to set clear boundaries between ourselves and others and to enjoy relationships — as much as we can — from a safe distance. Or maybe we should give ourselves to others, but only in moderation and only after we've developed enough security within ourselves to minimize whatever damage they may do to us.

In a world like ours, it's not unnatural to conclude that our best bet is to look after ourselves, to recover a sense of personal identity that was destroyed in our shame-based backgrounds, to value ourselves as worthwhile people no matter what anyone says or how we

6

might fail ("we're good people who sometimes do bad things"), and to present ourselves as worthy of acceptance and respect simply because we exist. Nothing matters more than restoring an enjoyable sense of who we are. That's the conclusion that much of modern culture has reached.

In the restoration process, we are often encouraged to draw on God's resources for help in bolstering our diminished self-esteem. The idea seems so Christian. We're hurting, having been damaged by dysfunctional backgrounds that did not faithfully reflect God's attitude toward us. So turn to Him to experience the power of His love that can heal our wounds and can give us back an enjoyable sense of ourselves. In this thinking, our worst problem, the one the gospel was intended to solve, is a failure to value ourselves as people whom God loves.

Now notice something very important. Once we start thinking that way, as soon as we view God primarily as an ally in the all-important battle to overcome our self-hatred, we will treat the Bible as little more than a revelation of God's determination to help us like ourselves more. Jesus' sacrifice on the cross, then, is valued as proof of our worth. God's love becomes the means by which we find release from shame. The Holy Spirit is reduced to a cheerleader who stirs us with excitement about our terrific potential. And the community of believers becomes, more than anything else, an opportunity for personal healing.

That is the reverse of the original plan. Now our relationship with ourselves becomes the centerpiece of our lives—thought about and worked on more than our relationship with God. He becomes a treasured resource for honoring what we see as our highest purpose (liking ourselves), and we worship Him for being so good to us, privately thinking that it is rather fitting for Him to do so. And we give ourselves to others in acts of responsible kindness, always being careful to become a victim of no one.

THE BIBLICAL PATTERN

But what I have just described is all wrong! The biblical pattern is very different.

God's design is that we relate in these ways:

- To *Him* by developing a confidence in His goodness that enables us to trust Him no matter what happens, a confidence born of an appreciation for His unmerited favor that is ours because of Christ's atonement for our sin.

- To *others* by giving ourselves away for Christ's sake with an energy that longs to see that same confidence in God grow in others.

- To *ourselves* by enjoying our unique dignity as men and women, who because of God's wisdom and kindness have something to give away that is useful for good purposes.

It is "another gospel" that invites us to change life around so that we relate to ourselves with an absorbing concern to enjoy our value, to others with self-protective caution, and to God with warm appreciation for extending Himself so that we can love ourselves. It is an approach to living that creates a never-ending concern with overcoming our problems. It begins a process of recovery that is never quite finished and, therefore, keeps our energy focused on our own well-being, defined as feeling good about who we are.

What I understand to be the biblical approach encourages us to view self-centeredness as a worse enemy than self-hatred. It invites us to explore the riches of Christ's value (rather than our own) by repenting of our failure to trust Him and learning to worship and serve Him because of His worth, not ours.

As we live our lives, we will either put ourselves first or we will live for God. And when problems arise, the differences between those two approaches will become especially visible. Either we will devote all our energies to overcoming our difficulties so that we can enjoy life again, or we will be more concerned to trust God in the midst of our problems so that we can better reflect His glory and serve His purposes.

THE PURPOSE OF THIS SERIES

Perhaps there is no more important principle to remember in handling life's problems than this: *Every difficulty in life – whether financial struggles, consuming self-hatred, or battles with addiction – presents us with an important opportunity to examine our relationships, to see where we've gotten off track in this priority area of life, and to find a way back.* If we try to solve our problems without looking at how we relate in the middle of them, we will live superficial lives that never reach their potential for glorifying God. And many difficulties will continue that have their (often unrecognized) foundation in wrong patterns of relating.

THE INSTITUTE OF BIBLICAL COUNSELING SERIES is a set of discussion guides or self-study booklets that address issues from the point of view of relationships. Each of the contributors takes a careful look at a common struggle (stress, self-image, guilt) and seeks to identify the ways people experiencing that struggle tend to approach relationships. Sometimes we just cannot see how we are relating that may create tension and generate emotional problems. In order to clearly identify how we are missing the mark of loving God and others (which would lead to appropriate self-acceptance), it can be helpful to understand the elements and attitudes within us that shape the ways we relate.

The purpose of my introduction to the series is to highlight the essential framework for understanding ourselves that the contributors assume in discussing their topics. Each contributor is an independent thinker who owes allegiance only to God's Word, but who also finds himself or herself in general agreement with ideas taught by the Institute of Biblical Counseling (IBC).

IBC is a training organization dedicated to thinking through an approach to handling life's problems that (1) builds entirely on biblical wisdom and (2) aims at restoring people to living as God designed us to live. Over the years, IBC has come to be identified with a unique understanding of people that continues to grow as we study, live, dialogue, and seek to help.

THE IBC PERSPECTIVE

Christians who affirm a similar commitment to God and His Word sometimes differ in their views of who we are and how we are supposed to approach relationships. Because of this, we thought it would be a good idea to outline the IBC framework for understanding people that is reflected in each of the booklets in this series.

IBC takes a position on a wide variety of subjects, each of which pertains to a theology of change: who we are, how we get in trouble, what needs to be changed, and how does God achieve His purposes in us. We are working toward the development of a theology of change that can guide churches in their ministry to hurting people, counselors as they work with individuals, small groups as they meet to share struggles and encouragement, and individuals who are serious about becoming more like Christ.

My intent in this brief discussion is far more modest than to present a comprehensive theology of change.[1] I hope to sketch only a partial view of people that might help us in our thinking about what is going on inside us as we approach our relationships. For the limited purposes of this study, I want to suggest *five basic ideas* about people.

1. People are RELATIONAL, not MECHANICAL.
2. People are PASSIONATE, not DUTIFUL.
3. People are THOUGHTFUL, not DRIVEN.
4. People are PURPOSEFUL, not REACTIVE.
5. People are (by nature) SELF-ORIENTED, not GIVING.

Those five ideas can be expressed in five more complete statements that will serve as an outline for this booklet.

Idea One
We are not mechanical things that can be fixed when broken; rather, we are *relational* persons who can be richly understood only by appreciating the deep longings within us that will never go away and that nothing but perfect relationship could satisfy.

Idea Two
We are *passionate* people in all that we do; every choice we make and every deed we do reflects the movement of a lively energy within us that conscious thought and choice do not fully direct. Like the Apostle Paul, we don't always do what we intend to do and we sometimes do what we've decided not to do (Romans 7).

11

Idea Three

We are *thoughtful* in our reactions to life; what we do is determined more by what we deeply (not always consciously) believe than by the external forces that influence us, including the impact of our family background.

Idea Four

We are *purposeful* in our choices; we are not programmed by past or present influences in any manner that relieves us of responsibility for the directions we choose. We move through life toward chosen goals that we think are reasonable and justified. Therefore, behavior can better be understood by looking at what it achieves than by studying its background.

Idea Five

By nature, we are entirely *self-oriented,* determined above all else to honor the final value of our well-being in a world where we trust no one else to look after us. Because we live with imperfect people, we assume that total trust would equal suicide. Devoting priority energy to looking after ourselves seems necessary and, therefore, moral. Our sinful commitment to looking after ourselves is always a more serious problem than the wounds we suffer at the hands of others.

Gaining a better understanding about these five points through this study will help you in your future discussions about what is going on inside you as you approach various aspects of relationships.

NOTE

1. There is a growing literature that reflects the IBC thinking about a number of concerns. See especially: *Inside Out, Men & Women, Understanding People,* and *The Marriage Builder* by Lawrence J. Crabb; *Encouragement* by Lawrence J. Crabb and Dan B. Allender; *The Wounded Heart* and *Bold Love* by Dan B. Allender; and *Parenting Adolescents* by Kevin Huggins.

CHAPTER ONE

PEOPLE ARE RELATIONAL, NOT MECHANICAL

ع

THE TROUBLE WITH FIXING PROBLEMS

When we probe beneath the surface of relationships into our attitudes toward ourselves and others, we discover that we tend to think of people (ourselves included) as little more than "useful things," which sometimes get broken and need to be fixed. Of course, we know better. We know that because we were created for relationships, we struggle with intangible realities that cannot be put back in order. To make relationships work, we need courage more than repair, and love more than insight. At some level, we all know that.

But still we approach the business of living in much the same way that a plumber inspects a leaky faucet: find the problem that is blocking proper functioning and fix it.

When people fail to provide us with what we want, we naturally assume that something is wrong with them that needs correction. And if the fault were fixed, one expects, they would treat us better and circumstances would move along more smoothly.

We send our kids to the counselor who specializes

in "adolescent problems" to repair whatever it is that makes them so stubbornly uncooperative. We go with our spouse to marriage counseling in order to help the counselor recognize what is blocking our mate from treating us more kindly. And, when problems in us cannot be denied, we're quite open to being shown that there is something twisted that therapy might straighten out.

When loneliness overwhelms us or anger consumes us, when passionate urges drive us relentlessly toward actions that we hate, when guilt is so strong that we can look no one in the eye, we immediately ask, "What's wrong?" Perhaps our psychological wires have gotten crossed in the confusion of a dysfunctional background, or maybe an emotional wound is festering beneath the surface of our consciousness and needs to be lanced by a discerning and skilled professional.

Perhaps there is a traumatic event in our past haunting us in a way that makes us run from anything that reminds us that it ever happened. Or maybe we're just stubborn people who need to be scolded, exhorted, and held accountable.

Whatever direction we move, the thinking is the same: *Figure out what's broken and fix it.* That's the way we naturally think. But that attitude reduces us to things like faucets that sometimes break and fail to function properly. And when that happens, when children bring home poor grades or when we lose our tempers too often, then someone with the necessary knowledge and appropriate skills needs to track down the root problem and repair it. The counseling industry is built largely on that idea. So, too, are many churches.

In modern culture, we have learned to depend on someone else's wisdom to help us identify the difficulty interfering with happy functioning: perhaps it is a demon plaguing us with powerful temptations or disturbing thoughts; or unacknowledged, unconfessed, and unforsaken sin; or sloppy spiritual habits that reflect no discipline. Or, if we're more psychologically oriented, we wonder if our troubles are caused by repressed trauma, infected wounds, or a crippling sense of low self-esteem.

Then we go to work, doing whatever it takes to resolve the problem in a way that returns us to normal living.

Each of the things I've mentioned can be, of course, a very real problem. Demons do trouble Christians, sin needs to be dealt with, disciplined living is important, and buried memories, internal pain, and self-hatred require helpful attention. But we are wrong to think of these things as "problems to be solved," like worn brakes on a car. If we do think of them that way, more basic concerns tend to be obscured.

THE STRUGGLE TO RELATE

All of our problems (unless they are medically caused) grow out of the struggle to relate well, with God, others, and ourselves. The central issue beneath our problems we must face is that they are always immediate—that is, they are present right now as we live. And they center on the attitudes within us toward ourselves and others and the energy with which we handle our relationships. Something about our existence as people in this world needs to be considered, something far deeper than our bad habits, crazy urges, or infected wounds.

Let me give an example. A young woman lost all interest in sex with her husband. Call that her "presenting problem," the concern that made her think that something was wrong and that she wanted to see changed. She had no idea why, after several years of an active and reasonably satisfying sex life with her husband, her desires for physical pleasure had fallen to near zero.

She, therefore, consulted a therapist to see what was wrong. The conclusion reached in therapy was that she was carrying around a load of unresolved guilt from premarital sexual activity (of which her husband knew nothing). The arousal she had recently felt, when her pastor seemed especially attentive to her, triggered a new surge of old guilt that was blocking desire for her husband.

She was encouraged to regard the arousal prompted by her kind pastor as normal, not to be acted on, of course, but still normal, and to forgive herself for past sinfulness by reminding herself that Jesus knew all about her past but had forgotten it since the day she confessed it years earlier. She then attended a "guilt recovery group" where she was repeatedly affirmed as a forgiven woman and strongly encouraged to live responsibly in light of God's tender love.

But six months of individual and group therapy hadn't helped. She felt better about herself but was no more interested in her husband. She decided that she must become more sexually aggressive at home. "If I really am a forgiven woman who has every reason to accept herself," she reasoned, "then I'll put that fact into action by choosing greater levels of cooperation in the bedroom."

She purchased sensual nightwear, paid more attention to her grooming, and surprised her husband with frequent physical overtures. But every time she did, she hated it—and she hated both her husband and herself as well. It just didn't work. Intercourse hurt. And worse, she felt like a prostitute.

Her next step in tracking down the problem was an appointment with a gynecologist. He assured her there was neither physical cause for the pain nor hormonal

reason for her lack of sexual desire. Upon his recom-
mendation, she scheduled time with another therapist:
a Christian woman who was trained to probe into the
complexities of a person's psychological make-up and
to bring the healing resources of Christ to bear on whatever wound might remain from a difficult childhood.
She agreed that there might be a trauma she hadn't
faced in her background — she suspected more severe
sexual abuse than she could remember — and, with the
help of the therapist, went looking for it.

After several months of failing in her search, she
thought about consulting a hypnotherapist who perhaps could help her "get to" even deeper regions of her
unconscious.

Right about that time, a friend from church who
was aware of her struggle gave her a book written by
a popular Bible teacher, denouncing all psychological approaches to healing as dangerously unbiblical.
Troubled Christians, this writer asserted, need only get
on their knees and spend more time in God's Word to
gain victory. Probing about in a mythical unconscious,
said the author, is a practice recommended by Freud,
not Scripture. Biblical counseling spends no time in the
past, little time with emotions, and much time focusing
on the need for deeper trust and more disciplined
obedience.

As a result of reading that book, she quit therapy,
feeling angry that her "Christian" therapist had so
badly misled her, and threw herself into prayer, Bible
study, and church activities.

Four months later, she collapsed. She wanted to
die. She still had no interest in a sexual relationship
with her husband, she felt angrily indifferent to her
pastor's efforts at encouragement, she had given up on
counseling, and felt bitter toward the church and God.

Earlier thoughts of suicide had always been checked
by concern for her children if she were to take her life.

Now she didn't care. All that mattered was escape from the intolerable burden of life. God had failed her. Counselors misled her. The church only added to her struggles. There was no way out but death.

What brought her to this terrible state? Why had she moved from a difficult presenting problem of reduced sexual desire to a desperate struggle with depression? Notice that in all her efforts to deal with her problem, she was looking for something wrong that could be fixed, something broken that if repaired would bring back an interest in relating physically with her husband.

She was treating herself as if she were a mechanical being, a machine that could break and be repaired, rather than as a relational being who fundamentally wanted (1) to receive what no one was offering and (2) to give deep parts of her womanhood to others that she had never given. She was running from a reality about life and about herself that not only terrorized her but also deepened a determination to somehow make her life work.

LONGING TO GIVE AND RECEIVE

Simply because she is a woman, created by God with the unique opportunities of womanhood, she yearned to be deeply enjoyed, to be prized and cherished in a way that would release the beauty in her soul that she knew was there but was too frightened to offer anyone.

Her father was a good man who had spent time with her and laughed with her and taken care of her. But somehow, in her words, "He had never connected with me." She added, "But I could never tell him that. It would have destroyed him. He had to see himself as a successful father whose three daughters all adored him. Once I told him that I wished we could talk more about hard issues in our relationship, and he got mad and sulked for weeks. I never asked him for anything again."

Can you hear the *terror* revealed in her words, a terror that perhaps there is no one who has the strength to be involved with her in the way she desires? And does the idea make sense that she would become *determined* to make it through life without ever facing that terror, perhaps by stubbornly refusing to give the part of her that she thinks no one can handle?

Her husband was also a good man, like her father — involved, patient, supportive, and affectionate. But again, she reported, "There was no connection." She felt that, in the core of her womanhood, she was neither penetrated by him nor released toward him. It isn't hard to see that their physical relationship was a replay of their personal relationship. She did not want to do anything that might require her to face the terror that she was unwanted and alone in the universe, and so, with clenched fists, she retreated from rich involvement with anyone.

She felt desperate for someone to move into her life, to touch her soul with liberating involvement that would give her the courage to more fully release to others all that could be enjoyed by them. But no one had, and she knew no one would — at least, not perfectly. She admitted, with considerable contempt toward both herself and others, "No one wants what I have to give."

With that rage-filled sentence, she began to move past the simple idea that something inside her was broken and needed to be fixed into the far richer thought that something is terribly flawed in all felt existence, including hers, and that she had no power to fix it. Like a fish in the desert, she yearned for what was not available.

As we all naturally do, she learned to despise those longings that had never been satisfied. She came to hate the "gills" of her feminine soul that were designed to draw life from the waters of rich connection, because those gills, rather than breathing happily in an ocean of strong love, continued only to gasp in pain. She found no water, only sand. And she was terrified that's all there was.

PAIN RELIEF

We do not want to believe that we are relational. It is so much easier to assume that beneath our desires for relating to others, we are really mechanical things that can be fixed if something goes wrong in our lives. To accept the truth that we are inescapably relational in a world where no one loves perfectly drives us to see that life, as we know it, is tragic. It forces us to admit that we are not safe.

The only sensible action in an unsafe, tragic world, we reason, is to devote our deepest energies to avoiding pain and to relieving whatever pain we cannot avoid. Ask the dentist for more Novocaine when the drill touches a nerve. Pull up the blanket on a chilly night. Walk away from a conversation with someone who is demeaning or, if possible, find a way to gain the upper hand. Work hard to be comfortable.

But despite our best efforts to avoid and relieve pain, a deep level of hurt remains that we cannot escape. If we maintain our commitment to minimize pain (a commitment served well by a mechanical view of ourselves), we will be required to numb our longings, to pretend we want less than we really do. And, at the same time we cut the nerves that cause us pain, we destroy all hope of joy.

It is true that we're never entirely successful in cutting off the nerve endings in our souls. At some level, we still desperately want what we were built to enjoy. So we sometimes smother the lingering evidence

20

of desire beneath whatever passion feels immediately stronger than the deeper longings within. And that effort leads either to depression or addiction. We become dull and relationally dead, or frantic and irresistibly drawn to whatever replaces pain with pleasure, if even for a moment.

We are relational, not mechanical. That means we hurt in ways that cannot be fixed. It also means that our only hope is to develop a relationship with someone who can support us in our pain, someone who will lift us to a sphere of living where something matters more than pain, until a day when we will hurt no more.

TERROR AND DETERMINATION

If we realize that we are relational beings, then the awareness of struggle in our lives will lead us to *evaluate the quality of our relationships* — our relationship with God, with others, and with ourselves. As we look in that direction (rather than searching for something to fix), we will be drawn into an awareness of a *paralyzing terror* and an *enraged determination*: "No one is doing for me what needs to be done, so I'll handle life on my own." When we enter the reality of terrifying aloneness, and when we sense the presence of a clenched fist that angrily declares our intention to survive, we will be either destroyed or drawn to God in a deepening relationship.

Handling the problems of life well requires that we wrestle with the central issues of our existence as people who were designed for perfect relationships that do not exist, except among the three Persons of the Trinity. Treating these issues as though they were either psychological packages of self-hatred or low self-esteem that can be unwrapped and fixed or spiritual deficiencies (like poor self-discipline) that can be corrected by mere effort will never help us come to grips with the central concerns of life. It will never lead us to that earnest search for God that is rewarded with the relationship our hearts desire.

We were created to enter into relationships and to enjoy them as our highest calling. To do so, we must learn what it means to face the terrors of existence in a life outside the Garden of Eden, where nothing is safe, and to realize how our tightly clenched fist waves in an angry determination to survive.

There is nothing broken to be fixed. But there is a terrible reality to be faced, a determination to be abandoned, and a new life to be discovered. We are relational, not mechanical.

CHAPTER TWO

PEOPLE ARE PASSIONATE, NOT MERELY DUTIFUL

ॐ

FLEEING ISOLATION

We will never really understand ourselves until we realize that we were designed for "relationship," connection—not merely good relationships, but perfect ones in which we give our best to other people in the happy confidence that they will enjoy what we give and be deeply blessed.

We were meant to find a quality of rest and pleasure in the company of others that is simply not available if we're alone. We, therefore, guard against whatever threatens to move us toward isolation. Rejection, criticism, indifference, manipulation—whatever threatens to separate us provokes deep fear.

And we fear those things with passion. We are drawn toward community with a deeply felt sense of attractive urgency. But because the kind of community we want is so rarely tasted, we tend to be more terrorized by the threat of isolation than warmed by the anticipation of love. We live with a passion-filled fear (*terror* is not too strong a word) that we are inescapably alone and an equally passion-filled determination to never feel the reality we fear.

To protect ourselves from feeling alone and unprotected in a hostile (or at best indifferent) world, we do precisely the wrong thing. We distance ourselves from whatever reminds us that isolation is a haunting reality by sealing ourselves away from people. We hide the part of us that is most frightened, those elements about our being that seem most needy and vulnerable to abandonment.

When we feel tender, we act gruff. When we're scared, we pretend confidence. When we're enraged, we are courteous, often in the name of commendable self-control. With careful discernment developed through countless encounters with hurt, we reveal to others what best serves our need to feel safe.

A moment's reflection makes clear that what we are doing is really futile: We isolate parts of ourselves in order to protect ourselves from isolation. That strategy is something like pulling out all our teeth to avoid decay or cutting off our feet to make sure no one steps on them. It is utterly self-defeating and foolish.

But — and here is the point to underline — *this strategy seems eminently reasonable and entirely justified when we're in the middle of doing it*. In our twisted way of thinking, retreating from a source of satisfaction because we might get hurt is the best plan we can come up with in a world where perfect relationship seems unavailable. We feel irrationally driven to keep away from the people who (we think) could destroy us even though we thereby create the very isolation we fear. But we can see no other choice.

The illusion of present safety seems better than the reality of certain death. So with feverish intensity, we work to keep ourselves away from personal danger and, at the same time, to block out the gnawing terror of isolation. We often succeed in smothering our terrors with simple denial — keeping busy or thinking about

24

something else. Some of us devise a more elaborate process of distancing ourselves that makes the terrors seem like they are bothering someone else. Or perhaps we solve the problem by relating to others with an intimidating anger that makes us feel in control of people and, therefore, not alone.

PASSIONATE INVOLVEMENT

It is important to realize that no amount of reasoning or persuading is powerful enough to make us change our course of action. At our deepest levels, in the decisions that count the most, we have moved beyond the reach of pressure. We have become more passionate than reasonable. *Only the intrusion of a person who can relieve our terror by providing us with both a guarantee of a perfect relationship and a taste of it now is a strong enough influence to help us shift directions. Only that person could persuade us that the terror is not real, thereby freeing us to give ourselves away with a reckless joy that laughs at every threat of abandonment.*

Passionate involvement is needed if passionate people are to really change to become all they can be. Let's be done with the shallow idea that good doctrine always leads to good living. And let's bury the still popular notion that pressure, whether forcefully applied by powerful leaders or subtly introduced through carefully timed expressions of hurt, moves people toward true holiness.

Something more (not less) than accurate teaching and consistent accountability is required to help us handle the problems of life. And that something more is *passionate involvement with God.* The Word of God is more than a handbook of doctrine and a set of prescriptions for proper living. It is alive just as the scribbled words on a Valentine's card from a faraway lover throb with vitality. Because we are passionate people terrified

25

of isolation, God's Word to us must be understood and embraced and shared with a passion stronger than all others.

But that rarely happens. In our culture, training in the Bible is too often dull. We tend to be precise but boring. We should be grieved and offended, but not surprised, when a senior seminary student at the top of his class is caught sneaking out of a pornographic film theater. We were built for passion, and if our souls are not stirred by Christ, then we'll arrange to have them stirred by something else. That seminary student will be changed only by discovering the passion of knowing Christ in a way that exposes its sensual counterfeit as a pathetic, short-lived, and costly imitation.

We have managed to take the only really living Book and squeeze the life out of it with an exacting exegesis that engages the brain but not the relationship-starved soul, and then we arrange the remaining dust into neat little piles that we call theology — the study of God. How utterly terrible!

That process of robbing Scripture of life encourages Christians to pursue one of two courses in handling their problems. Since a passion that reaches into the deeply felt but often hidden terrors of isolation apparently is not available, Christians choose *either* to kill their passion with the weapons of orthodoxy and moral respectability ("I'm doing fine. I can defend my millennial position, and I've never had an affair") *or* to handle their problems by injecting their theology with whatever makes them feel meaningfully alive, perhaps a fascinating preoccupation with their own inner workings or an absorbing focus on devastating memories or a thrilling excursion into sensual indulgence.

Those in the first group keep defending themselves and defining what they believe and try hard to sense that it makes a real difference. Those in the second group worship God (if at all) with a strange intensity that seems more an exhibit of themselves than a pre-occupation with Someone bigger.

But neither course is necessary. There is a way out of our dilemma that puts us in touch with the sheer non-boringness of God and, at the same time, takes into account the deepest passions of human existence. It is a way that sees God as someone different from either a military commander who values duty above all else or a kindly grandfather who loves to see the kids having a good time. We must learn to see God as the only Person who can relieve the terror of isolation with His powerful and good presence, the only One who can melt our determination to survive isolation by enticing us with the joys of involvement.

COURAGE AND HUMILITY

The beginning of that way out of our dilemma comes when we find (1) the *courage to admit our terror*, entering it fully without requiring relief, and (2) the *humility to face our arrogant determination*, admitting our foolish attempts to survive are an affront to God. The point of this chapter is easily stated: We are terrified, determined people whose terror is unnecessary and whose stubborn determination is wrong. The terrors of aloneness can be replaced with faith and trust and hope; and our determination to survive can give way to rest and joy and love.

But these wonderful things will never happen until we set our sights higher (certainly not lower) than obeying God merely out of a sense of duty and envision the possibility of passionately giving ourselves to Him and, for His sake, to others.

We are designed for passionate obedience, not dutiful compliance. And the only passion that is strong enough to support consistent obedience is gladness, never fear. To know this passion requires that we experience God as good even in the middle of the unrelieved terror that comes as we face the ugliness of our proud determination.

I just received word that a fifty-six-year-old pastor has left his wife for the church secretary. After thirty-three years of marriage, with no history of infidelity, this highly respected Bible teacher yielded to sinful passions within him that apparently were more compelling than whatever passion he may have felt for his wife, children, church, reputation, or God.

This man knows the Bible. He knows his decisions are wrong; he frequently has taught on the biblical route to defeating sin. There is little he can be told that he doesn't already know. What, then, should be our response to this man—and to ourselves when we battle against similar passions within us capable of shipwrecking our testimony?

We've all heard similar stories, too many times. Usually, if it involves someone we don't know or don't like, we feel offended by the obvious immorality and, with head-wagging self-righteousness, wonder, "How can people do such terrible things?" If, however, the person is a friend or an acquaintance whom we do like, our reaction tends to be more perplexed: "I can't understand what was going on inside that person to cause him to do something like that. I wish I could help."

We tend to be far more tolerant when people we know do bad things, unless, of course, the offender is a parent, spouse, child, or sibling. Then we swing wildly back and forth between an enraged moralism with a distinctly selfish ring to it ("How could you do this to me?") and a desperate desire to help ("What can I do to help? I'll do anything!").

But what is the best response to this pastor? If we could sift through our own tangled emotions and, with the discerning intensity of Christ, get down to the real issues in his heart, I suspect we might recognize two ingredients making up the soil in which the seeds of immorality took root and grew: a *terror* that there is no one in the universe good enough or strong enough to connect with him at the level his desperate soul requires and a *determination* to find a way to create for himself the illusion that what he wants is, after all, available.

Like all of us, this man is more strongly driven by passions than directed by reason. Neither an appeal to his mind through education nor a challenging exhortation to his soul will do much to generate the kind of repentance that could deeply shift the direction of his life. The most profound level of change requires that the most primitive passions of his heart be exposed and entered. Then, in the midst of the shattering agitation that necessarily follows, he must cry out to God as his only hope.

Because terror and determination, in my understanding, are the core passions of the natural human soul, let me briefly clarify their meaning in the remainder of the chapter.

TERROR: THE PASSION THAT MAKES US HIDE

A single woman, age twenty-eight, had offended nearly everyone in her community of friends. When, at the urging of one particularly close friend, she came to see me, she knew that her relationships were a mess. But she insisted with considerable force that the blame be divided between herself and the insensitivity of others.

Ten minutes into our first session, she tilted her pretty head to one side, then arranged her mouth into a smile that looked more like a sneer, and said, "I just want you to know that I don't trust you—and I don't really see why I should."

I replied, "Trusting anyone would scare you to death."

That comment, after twenty more minutes of parrying, opened her to talking tearfully about her most passionate fantasy—a wonderfully terrifying day-dream in which she trusted someone with good results. In her mind, she imagined that her father invited her to dinner at a quietly elegant restaurant, and reaching across the linen tablecloth, he rested his hand warmly on hers, looked tenderly and purposefully into her eyes, and said, "I want to hear everything that's happening in your life. I want to know you."

As she described her fantasy (and it was just that; her father could not reasonably be expected to ever involve himself so meaningfully with his daughter), she softened from a nasty, sneering bully into a fright-ened, troubled young woman. When I pointed out the transformation to her, she said, "Why do I feel so afraid whenever I sense something beautiful in me?"

This woman was gripped by terror, a paralyzing fear that if she ever presented herself to people as the scared, desperate person she was, no one would be willing to bear the weight of her desires. She would be abandoned, left alone. And worse, if she offered kindness to another, which she sometimes wanted to, it might be met with polite indifference.

Remember the thought that began this chapter: We long for perfect relationship in which we give our best to others in the happy confidence that they will enjoy what we give and be blessed by it. My client was terrified that no one would ever accept her with all her ugliness and stay involved long enough to draw out her potential to be a richly delightful and enjoyably strong woman.

That's the terror we all feel. Is God really good? Is He up to the job of staying involved with us? Does He care enough to protect us against the harmful influences of life and bring us through as wonderfully satisfied, happily passionate people? When we knock on the door of the universe, is anyone home— anyone, that is, who is stronger than every enemy and good enough to be entirely trusted with our souls?

The evidence of life is not terribly reassuring. Bad things sometimes happen that God obviously doesn't prevent, and He rarely does much to cushion the blow. And we wonder: Is He really good?

Then we worry. If God isn't good, we are entirely alone because certainly no one else is perfectly good. We are left to face a coldly indifferent world without anyone to encourage us. We remain alive with a desire for love and affirmation that only community can provide; but if God isn't good, then there is no community capable of providing what we need. We are alone, with no one to meaningfully help with our fears of inadequacy, "unlovability," pointlessness.

That fundamental terror lies beneath all our relational problems and psychological symptoms. It is a terror that must be faced rather than avoided because the richest experience of God that convinces us we are not alone comes to us only in the terror. For those who manage to insulate themselves from the terror behind walls of denial, superficiality, and temporary pleasures, the words "Be still, and know that I am God" mean very little (Psalm 46:10).

DETERMINATION:
THE PASSION THAT MAKES US HATE

Nothing feeds determination like terror. Something in us feels offended that God doesn't do a more convincing job of proving His goodness to us: getting us out of financial trouble, making our kids turn out right, giving us better friends. The unrelieved terror that no one will help us makes us feel justified in doing whatever we can to arrange for our own well-being.

The young woman mentioned earlier had become hateful toward others, especially those who went out of their way to be kind to her. Kindness moved her toward facing her terror. Her internal response to kindness was to say, "You're kind, but not kind enough. No one is. I hate you for even trying. You're just teasing me with a little taste of what I can never have. Let me go back to the power of hatred. At least there's some satisfaction in knowing I am powerful enough to upset others. But when I do upset you, I hate myself as well. Just leave me alone. Stop being kind."

Our determination to look after ourselves is a deeply felt passion that seems entirely reasonable—not on theological grounds, but because it seems to be our only chance for survival. And the root sinfulness behind that determination is the ongoing suspicion that God is not good enough to fully trust with our lives.

Ever since Adam and Eve failed to remain within boundaries that God had set with their happiness in mind, each of their descendants has succumbed to the same temptation: to believe that God is not good, that there is no relief in Him from the terror of isolation, that we are therefore justified in doing whatever relieves pain and makes life more immediately comfortable.

We are passionately determined people—determined to make life work for us. And when it doesn't, we hate God for doing so little to cooperate, we hate others for their indifference, and we hate ourselves for not being able to arrange for our comfort.

In handling life's problems, we must take into account the passions deep within us that reflect our terror and determination. It won't do merely to prescribe a stronger commitment to duty and to reinforce that prescription with biblical facts. Only by facing our terror and admitting our selfish determination will we ever find the deep joys of passionate trust and obedience. We are passionate, not merely dutiful.

CHAPTER THREE

PEOPLE ARE THOUGHTFUL, NOT DRIVEN

ॐ

HATING YOU, HATING ME

Since the Fall, no one naturally thinks God is good. The strong suspicion that He is not worth trusting is the disease with which Adam infected the entire human race. As children of Adam, each of us has turned away from God to find life; we have depended on ourselves and others for the satisfaction with Him we were created to enjoy. And we turn away with angry passion, determined to make it on our own, without God.

With equal passion, but of a different kind, we turn toward others, desperately hoping we can find in them contentment to end our terror of aloneness. But it never quite works. Even the best relationships lack something. We become aware of our disappointment, gradually, until the terror reawakens within us that perhaps we really are alone — and without hope.

At that point, when terror is creeping into our souls, our already entrenched hatred for God spills over to other people. When we start hating, we like it. Hatred feels so much more powerful than terror, and we often nurture it to avoid feeling what makes us seem so little.

The more we allow ourselves to feel angry, the more justified it seems. After all, if God really did create us and if He wants us to trust Him, then why does He leave us to suffer at the hands of uncaring parents and mean school teachers and abusive neighbors and competitive, jealous siblings? It doesn't take long for our anger to boil toward God and toward the people in our lives who have hurt us the most.

But to admit that no one in our lives is giving us what we need nudges us closer to the fear that we're committed to never facing: We really are alone. And worse, to admit fully our disappointment in others might even tempt us to reconsider our attitude toward God: He may be our only hope.

As soon as we lean in that direction, however, something inside us reflexively puts up a fight. Above everything else, we are committed to not trusting God.

We therefore resort to a more sophisticated strategy for bolstering our confidence that our lives can work without God: *We blame ourselves for the failure of others.* We're bad, not them. They would have come through for us if only we had been more desirable or competent. The little girl acted seductively toward her uncle; that's why he molested her. She felt an enjoyment when he gently touched her that was wrong to feel. It's her fault for feeling it. So the real problem in the little girl's world is within her, not him.

That's how she thinks. It's safer. Blaming herself for the abuse allows her to still believe her uncle is a good man, like other men. She's the bad one, not him! Thinking that way restores hope that if she could become less seductive, if she would manage to not be aware of sensual feelings, then people might treat her well—and life would work.

In my understanding, that is a common origin of the self-hatred we hear so much about today. Many pastors and counselors assume that self-hatred is the worst problem we have. If we can just learn to like ourselves better, then we will be able to handle whatever comes our way.

But learning to like ourselves leaves three more basic problems unresolved: (1) We still hold it against people for not coming through for us; (2) we still are determined to find our life in people and things; and (3) we still refuse to be on speaking terms with God.

Think of these four problems (the three just mentioned plus self-hatred) as a "dynamic structure" on which we build our lives:

- *Fury toward God:* He's not good enough to trust.

- *Dependence on others:* Someone has to come through for me.

- *Anger at the primary people in our lives:* Of all people, I thought you would have been there for me.

- *Anger at ourselves,* for whatever it is about us that makes everyone turn away: What's wrong with me? Even my own father rejects me!

With those elements in place, we take on the job of living. All the descendants of Adam and Eve develop their own unique version of this same basic structure as they move through their experience of life.

STYLES OF RELATING

Notice that the root of the entire structure is a passionate disbelief in the goodness of God. If that could be replaced with humble confidence in His flawless kindness, the whole structure would collapse. But the suspicion that God isn't good is the deepest reality in our natural make-up and, therefore, the most difficult to change.

Only supernatural power can disrupt suspicion and create confidence. *We offer only superficial healing if we deal with self-hatred, hatred of others, and preoccupying neediness without also exposing our deep rage at God for not being good on our terms.* If we fail to take into account the struggle to trust God with our final and immediate well-being, we cannot call our efforts to help truly biblical.

With that central conviction undisturbed, and the rest of the structure firmly in place, we set out on the search for a way to make life work. We know we can't trust God, we are determined to find happiness elsewhere, and we feel cautious about what we give to people — we might be rejected.

Given these boundaries, we come up with a strategy for handling life that makes sense to us when we evaluate what we've seen so far. We develop a *style of relating* to people that moves us away from our terror of isolation and toward the hoped for community.

The specific style we select depends on how we size up both ourselves and other people, whether it be:

■ Aloof and retiring

■ Intimidating and powerful

■ Genial and agreeably sociable

■ Aggressive and achievement-oriented

We arrive at thoughtful (wrong, but well thought out) conclusions about three things that matter to us very much: (1) What can people do to either damage me or make me feel good? (2) What is there about me that people are likely to criticize or respect? (3) What do I have that people sometimes want? *The conclusions we reach, not the experiences of life, guide us as we decide how best to get along in our unique world.*

Notice in my argument so far that there are two levels at which our thinking is important. The first is the foundational level where we angrily refuse to trust God. The second is the more immediately practical level where we figure out how to maneuver through relationships with the least damage and the most joy. It is that second level that I want to consider in this chapter.

EXPLORING STORIES

Each of us has a story to tell, a long and fascinating story that includes happiness, pain, satisfaction, frustration, dreams, nightmares, love, rejection, excitement, discouragement, tenderness, and abuse. If we tell our stories to one another without rushing, and if we listen carefully, we can begin to understand the ways we think about life. Let me illustrate.

Jim, a middle-aged husband and father, struggled with a chronic fear of failure. He performed well on his job, but constantly worried that his superiors wouldn't be pleased. Years of reassurance and adequate performance ratings didn't help.

His wife, Lori, did her best to understand his struggles, but the endless repetition of self-deprecating remarks had worn her patience thin. Jim felt reasonably secure in his relationship with Amy, their seven-year-old daughter, but he had a hard time carrying on even a casual conversation with his fourteen-year-old son, Todd. He couldn't stop worrying that one day Todd would get into serious trouble.

One evening the police knocked on their door and wanted to ask Todd some questions about a robbery at a local convenience store. There was no firm evidence linking Todd to the robbery, but the conversation with the policemen made it clear that Todd was hanging around with an undesirable crowd.

When the officers left, Jim fell apart. Rather than speaking directly with Todd about his concerns, he retreated into his bedroom and sobbed for half an hour. Lori lost her composure. For the first time in twenty-one years of marriage, she lashed out at him with all the frustration that had built up every time Jim had retreated from responsibility. "No wonder the boy is in trouble," she shouted to conclude her harangue. "He hasn't got a man for a father!"

That event brought Jim into counseling. In our first session, he never lifted his eyes to meet mine for more than a few seconds. Fighting back tears as he spoke, Jim told me the story of the policemen's visit, his retreat to the bedroom, and Lori's explosion. When he finished, he quietly added, "I know she's right about how weak I sometimes am, but I don't think she understands how bad I feel about myself. I really wish I could do better."

Notice three things in Jim's two sentences. First, the word *sometimes*. Is it possible that Jim is saying he sometimes is weak but at other times he's strong, or at least less weak — "and Lori never seems to notice that!" Second, "I don't think she understands how bad I feel." I hear in those words an angry demand that Lori give him something he thinks he deserves, and an assumption that until *someone* (Lori is a logical choice) gives him understanding, he really cannot be stronger. Third, "I really wish I could do better." With that sentence, he shifts the responsibility to me to help him do better. I'm now required to do whatever counselors do that will free him to live more effectively.

I wanted to help Jim. I wanted to relate to him in a way that would be useful to God's purpose in his life. In order to do so, it was helpful to review what I know about the structure beneath his approach to life.

I know Jim is a *relational* man who, because he is

a man, longs to make a legitimate impact on his world and to be recognized and valued as a person who can do so. I also know that apart from God Jim has no hope of ever experiencing that kind of deep satisfaction. And because something in him (the same thing is in me) resists coming to God, he must be terrorized that one day he'll wake up and realize his life amounts to nothing, and there is no one to help. But, and I also know this, he is determined to find some way to arrange for the satisfaction he so badly wants. His terror and his determination coupled with his relational nature, make Jim a passionate man.

Now, listen to a few snapshots of the story he told me in subsequent sessions. Prick up your ears whenever you hear any of the following:

- How he was disappointed.

- What it was about him that disappointed others.

- What he thinks he could offer that would persuade others to relieve his terror of isolation by being involved with him.

JIM TELLS HIS STORY — A CONDENSED VERSION

I was the third of three kids, the only boy. Dad was a tough sort of guy, the kind who could do anything. A man's man. He had to take over responsibility for his younger brother, Blake, when their father died. Dad was about fifteen when that happened, and Blake was maybe eight or nine. So Dad became a combination big brother and father to him.

Dad learned to survive by sheer hard work and resourcefulness. He taught his brother how to do plumbing work—I have no idea where Dad learned

39

it—and by the time Blake was thirteen he was making extra money for the family with small plumbing jobs in the neighborhood.

Dad was really proud of Blake. I think I heard that story a hundred times. Blake is now a successful building contractor—has been for years.

My two sisters are a lot older than me. I came along when they were twelve and nine. Dad was thrilled finally to have a son, and my sisters were excited to have a baby brother. I think I was more like a doll to them than a brother. They fussed over me a lot—too much I think. But they meant no harm.

I was a pretty decent athlete, mostly baseball, but I was good at most sports I tried. Dad liked to come to my games when he could, but he wasn't much into sports. Never had time when we were kids. He mostly liked to work with his hands. But I just didn't have a knack for building or mechanical things. Still don't.

I was an average student. My two sisters both went to college. One completed a two-year secretarial course; the other has a degree in advertising. They're both married now and neither one is employed. We didn't have much money back then. I think my parents were hoping I'd get a scholarship, but I didn't. So I worked my way through a local community college—took an associate degree in business and accounting. I've been working in middle management now for nearly ten years—doing okay, not getting rich, but most of the bills are paid.

I met my wife when we were both about twenty. She had just come off a bad breakup, and I had never dated much. When I asked her out, I think she accepted just to keep from being lonely. But that's okay. She seemed to like me all right, and I liked her. We dated for about three years, then decided to get married when she was offered a transfer job to another city with the

40

company she was working for then. It would have been a pretty big promotion. But she decided to marry me instead.

It's never been a bad marriage. At least I didn't think so till the other night when Lori really yelled at me. I guess I've completely messed things up.

❖ ❖ ❖

LOOKING AT JIM'S STORY

Even that condensed version of Jim's story is full of suggestive material that could help us understand the strategy he has chosen to handle life. I will select only a few elements that relate to the three categories already mentioned.

How Was He Disappointed?
The one area in which Jim performed above average — sports — was an area in which his father had little interest. His dad, described by Jim as a "man's man," apparently defined masculinity in terms of plumbing skills and similar talents, which Jim lacked. Jim was deeply disappointed by the failure of his father to richly affirm something within him that was worthy of respect. His treatment by his sisters as a "doll" did nothing to help his sense of masculine identity.

What Was It About Him That Disappointed Others?
Two things stand out clearly from the narrative: academic mediocrity (no scholarship) and a lack of mechanical aptitude provoked a response in his father that was painful for Jim. It is a reasonably safe deduction to suggest that Jim came to believe that taking hold of responsibilities was pointless. He would never receive recognition for a job well done. His style of courting Lori reflects his conviction that aggressive involvement would not be rewarded.

41

What Could He Offer to Relieve His Sense of Aloneness?

From living in his particular home, Jim concluded that he had nothing strong to offer anyone. It's possible that his happiest memories were those times when his sisters doted on him. (Exactly how they did that is a matter worthy of further inquiry.) From the data presented, it is reasonable to wonder if Jim had decided that presenting himself to others as helpless gave him his best chance of feeling connected with someone.

With these observations in mind, we can suggest that Jim's overriding conclusion was that he needed to be understood by someone tender and warm to have any hope of happiness. In his thinking, taking hold of his life was futile. It would be met with scorn. In those areas where he had to perform, he was always terrified that he would fall short of standards. When challenges came his way he retreated into a well-rehearsed plea that no one expect more of him than he could deliver.

Jim had reached certain conclusions about other people and himself. These conclusions then guided him to select a style of relating that never took risks, kept out of the limelight, and begged for understanding when life was overwhelming.

Changing that style of relating requires more than exhorting Jim to take hold of his world. It requires more than identifying the wrong beliefs beneath his strategy of weakness, articulating right ones, and encouraging him to remind himself of the right ones until he "really believes" them.

In the early years of IBC, I was identified with a school of thought known as *cognitive therapy*. According to the ideas of that school, the root issues behind "presenting problems" always involved irrational, incorrect beliefs that needed to be exposed, challenged, and replaced.

I find the cognitive approach inadequate—helpful,

42

but perhaps a bit shallow. Much more needs to be done than merely to change our conscious beliefs by drilling new ones into our heads. We must be open to facing the pain and struggle in those events that shaped our beliefs. We must have the courage to enter the terrors of isolation that an uninvolved or critical parent triggered within us.

When we feel the energy attached to our beliefs and are willing to evaluate the wisdom (or foolishness) of our beliefs while we are feeling the pain, then our thinking can be meaningfully changed. In the context of feeling our terror and confessing our determination, we can more easily recognize that our beliefs were not merely unfortunate cognitive accidents, but were rather useful tools in serving the passionate purpose in our hearts to make life work without God. Repentance then becomes a meaningful possibility.

We are responsible people. God holds us accountable for what we do precisely because we are *not* hopelessly driven by forces set in motion by our dysfunctional backgrounds. We are thinking people who figure out how we will make life work apart from God. We are thoughtful, not driven.

CHAPTER FOUR

PEOPLE ARE PURPOSEFUL, NOT REACTIVE

ð

VICTIMS OR AGENTS?

Suppose I were to hit you with neither cause nor warning. If, in your startled anger, you hit me back, would your punch be a reflexive action triggered by mine, or would it be a choice?

Would your answer to that question change if part of the triggering event had taken place years before the response? For example, if your father sexually abused you when you were a little girl, and if three decades later your husband left you for another woman, would your decision to never again be involved with a man be a reaction, fully understandable and morally acceptable given your inability to choose another direction, or a choice for which you bear responsibility?

The same issue can be raised another way. Although the courts of our land might rule your punch as legitimate self-defense and, therefore, not blameworthy; and although your counselor would perhaps understand your determination to avoid risk with men as a reasonable outcome of your background—how would God think about these things? Would He view your punch as a provoked choice, but at some level, still a choice that you made, or would He somehow blame me for your punch? Would He take the modern view that your man-avoiding decision reflects the emotional wound of shame that needs healing? Or would He judge you as a hurting but stubborn woman more committed to your own protection than to another's blessing? Would He say you were wrong? Or that you needed help?

The question is important. If your actions are as inevitable and unchosen as gasping for air when your head is being held underwater, then He would move toward you as Helper. But if you have chosen one path (a wrong one) when you could have chosen another, then He would stand before you as Judge.

Which would He do? Are we victims or agents? Do we merely react to what happens to us, particularly if it is severely painful? Or do we select a course of action according to our understanding of what best serves our values in the midst of our circumstances? Do we move through life like sailboats shifting direction with the wind? Or are we free moral agents who consistently pursue chosen purposes no matter how hard the wind may be blowing?

The question is not easily answered. If we say we are more fundamentally victims than agents, we cut out the moral basis for responsibility and make God unreasonable when He judges. Christ's sacrifice on the cross is then reduced to a benign expression of love that can encourage us to assert our value as we endure rejection. Without a strong view of human responsibility, the crucified Christ loses His identity as Redeemer and becomes little more than a tragic martyr.

But if we insist that we function as free agents no matter what occurs in our lives, then we are in danger of becoming harshly insensitive to legitimate pain as people struggle to live properly in the face of sometimes overwhelming hurt. The cross, then, may be used to increase the burden of responsibility and to suffocate us with pressure. Christ may be seen as more of a stern moralist than a compassionate Priest.

Perhaps there is a path in the middle of the two extremes, a way of sympathetically recognizing the damage done to us as victims that does not exempt us from the deepest levels of responsibility. Although we are not *fundamentally* reactive, maybe our capacity to move with chosen purpose leaves room for those times in life when we feel powerless to move in a direction other than the one in which we find ourselves moving.

In this chapter, I want to suggest a three-tier model of understanding our freedom as agents. At the deepest level of our being, we move in a direction that we choose. At a second level, we experience the effects of how we are treated by others, and those effects either strengthen or weaken our chosen core direction. At a third level, the level of everyday living, our actions feel either chosen or necessary — depending in part on whether we are aware more of the basic *directions* we have chosen or the *wounds* that encourage that direction. Let me explain further.

VICTIMS FIRST, THEN AGENTS

The rise of the codependency movement has elevated the status of legitimate victimization to unreasonable heights. "Don't blame the victim" has become a rallying cry to motivate us to accept people in their woundedness and to help them find the courage to begin the painful process of healing.

Our inner child, say the experts, has been so severely shamed, suffocated, and sterilized that we feel no option but to hide our true self and to parade whatever false self holds the promise of winning approval. Notice

47

in this thinking that shame, defined as feelings of unworthiness put there by bad treatment from others, is central. There is no deeper level where responsibility resides.

But in the context of group support, we can find the courage to reclaim our identity as *valuable* people and to assert ourselves as *free* people who no longer need to be trapped in the role of victims.

The harmful effects of a dysfunctional background define our victimization. If someone cuts you with a knife, you bleed. If your father is an alcoholic, you develop identity struggles. In both cases, you are a victim. The thing to do, of course, is not to resign yourself passively to living as a damaged victim. Dress your wounds. Reclaim your identity. Nourish your inner child. Do something about the damage. Restore the integrity of your cut body and your injured soul by doing whatever it takes to promote healing.

It is in the act of restoring personal wholeness that you come to know yourself as an agent, a separate, strong, valuable, intact *self*. In this view, the primary function of being an agent is to *restore what was taken from you in your victimization*.

That is a "two-tier" model: The wounds inflicted on us as victims make up the primary level, and our capacity to find wholeness as agents defines the second level.

We might call this the *victims first, then agents* view.

Primary Level: We are *victims*:
- vulnerable to hurt,
- damaged by life.

Secondary Level: We are *agents*:
- capable of courageously asserting ourselves to overcome the damage

inflicted on us by others and to rise above our identity as victims.

AGENTS FIRST, THEN VICTIMS

In another view, agency is seen as more basic than victimization. If we define agency as the capacity (and therefore the responsibility) to do what is right regardless of our background and circumstances, then victimization is reduced to secondary status. Certainly we are all victims of injustice, some more severely than others, and it is right to extend sympathy and provide help whenever we can to hurting people.

But, in this view, we must never permit the injustice we've suffered, no matter how severe, to serve as an excuse for irresponsible living. Nothing should be emphasized above our duty to live by God's standards and our ability in Christ to do so. A sense of legitimate identity, to whatever degree it is important, will be recovered as we use our agency not to seek fulfillment but to live as we should. The primary function of being agents is not to heal our identity but to *exercise our responsibility*.

Call this the *agents first, then victims* view.

Primary Level: We are *agents*:
- capable of choice,
- inclined to sin, but able to choose holiness in Christ's strength.

Secondary Level: We are *victims*:
- vulnerable to hurt,
- damaged by life, but not in a way that eliminates our capacity to make right choices.
  Legitimate healing comes through responsible living.

49

TWO EXTREMES

Which view is correct? Do we transcend how we've been injured by using our energy to find ourselves? Or should we exercise our capacity for holy living by making godly choices in dependence on Christ, and thereby rob personal struggles of the power to interfere with God's purposes for us?

By insisting that complexity be reduced to manageable levels, our culture presents us with these two options:

1. *Victims first, then agents:* Highlight our victimization, then appeal to our power as agents to assist with healing.
2. *Agents first, then victims:* Emphasize our agency as the capacity for moral living regardless of background or circumstances.

In recent years, we've made huge strides in understanding how dysfunctional families inflict horrible damage on the human soul and how that damage can be repaired. It's almost impossible to recommend one or two key books on the subject because there are so many. But we've stood relatively still in thinking about the depths of our dignity (and culpability) as agents who are called and, therefore, responsible to reflect the kind and holy character of God. We still think about responsibility mostly at the behavioral level: "Okay, I know your wife is awful and your mother is domineering, but you must remain faithful as a husband and loyal as a son anyway."

The effect of our deep awareness of woundedness and our shallow understanding of sin has been to identify compassion with the *victims first, then agents* view and to associate stern judgmentalism with the *agents first, then victims* view. Those who emphasize damage to the soul are thought of as caring and sensitive (or soft on sin, as seen from the position that highlights agency). Those who focus on responsibility are seen as harsh and legalistic (unless viewed with a similar focus, then they are held up as God-centered defenders of the faith).

My purpose in this chapter is to assume a rich awareness of damage and to promote a deeper view of responsibility—a view that will focus on the choices we make at the level of our core purpose.

TRULY VICTIMS, BUT AGENTS FIRST AND LAST

It is helpful here to remember what has already been discussed in earlier chapters. We are *relational* (chapter 1), *passionate* (chapter 2), and *thoughtful* (chapter 3):

- We yearn for what can be found only in a perfect relationship with someone infinitely good and infinitely powerful.

- Because we're not convinced that anyone like that really exists (the evidence presented to our senses is not persuasive), we are terrified of remaining forever alone and unsatisfied. In our terror, we become determined, with all the passion of a drowning man about to go under for the third time, to find some way to survive our isolation.

- We choose strategies for survival that reflect our evaluation of God, ourselves, and others.

The next element in our understanding of people—and it overlaps and naturally flows out of what we've studied so far—is *purposefulness*. Let me indicate the direction of my thinking by defining a central idea: *We chart a course for ourselves in life that depends entirely*

51

on our ability to choose. The most central decision we make, whether to honor God as good in all that we do or to look out for ourselves in a lonely world, depends on the energy of choice within us, not the quality of circumstances that surround us. We are therefore more purposeful as agents than wounded as victims.

However, to avoid becoming shallow and harsh in our attitude toward hurting people, we must never minimize the extent of human anguish. The damage we suffer at the hands of others is real — we are victims. But that damage neither creates our chosen purpose nor alters it when it is wrong. It will never make a bad purpose good or a good one bad.

The natural purpose of every fallen human heart is the same: to restore the *self* to the joys of relationships and meaning. Given our stubborn belief that God is not good enough to trust fully (if we believe He exists at all), no other purpose could appear reasonable to relational, passionate, thoughtful creatures.

Life's experiences will only strengthen that natural purpose until the revelation breaks through that God is good enough to accept rebellious children into His family, and that He is loving enough to find a way to do so without compromising His utterly righteous standards. But until that truth completely seizes our souls (and it never will, not completely, until Heaven), we will in at least some measure honor that wrong purpose as we live.

Precisely how we honor it will depend on the particular kind and severity of damage we experience. Someone subjected to satanic ritual abuse may scramble to survive in a way that creates the pattern of relating known as a multiple personality disorder. Someone whose family was loving and stable may go on to a successful career (as a dentist, corporate executive, or pastor). In each case, the underlying purpose may be the same: preserving, protecting, and enhancing the *self*.

The energy behind that purpose, we must realize, is our frantic demand that the terrors of isolation be avoided and that life work — a demand that feels entirely justified and moral. But we must also see that, although one choice may feel compulsive and unhealthy (leading to severe problems) and the other may feel chosen and adaptive, both reflect a strong degree of compulsiveness. To the person making the choice, they both seem necessary because they grow out of the same passionate determination to survive in a friendless world. It's easier to see ourselves as agents at the primary level of basic life direction (toward God or self), than at the secondary level of reaction to the quality of life.

Folks who handle rejection by retreating into people-pleasing compliance will experience themselves as neurotic; their style of relating seems to them both self-defeating and thoroughly unchosen. They feel trapped. But when people meet rejection with assertive independence and a brave willingness to engage in other relationships — a choice they make perhaps because their background includes more affirmation — they will sense that their style of relating is healthy and courageously chosen.

But both reactions are really immoral if they reflect a determination to survive, using available resources, that is rooted in a lack of confidence in God's goodness. As people who at core are agents, we move purposefully through our world, passionately committed, above every other purpose, to avoiding loneliness and finding life. And in so doing, we supremely insult the God who has told us that life is a free gift, undeserved but available to those who, by trusting in Christ, will shift their direction from finding themselves to resting in Him.

The position I hold could be called *truly victims, but agents first and last.*

Primary Level: We are *agents* responsible for whether or not we trust God as good and, therefore, live to take care of ourselves or to glorify Him.

Secondary Level: We are truly *victims* vulnerable to damage from mistreatment that affects our view of ourselves and others, that strengthens our conviction that God is not good, and that further justifies our determination to take care of ourselves.

Tertiary Level: We are *agents* responsible for the specific strategies we select in order to survive.

PETER'S AFFAIR

Perhaps an illustration will clarify the main points of this chapter.

A successful businessman named Peter, about to take early retirement at age fifty-five, was well known for his gruff, almost ruthlessly impersonal style of relating. He had made plenty of money but very few friends.

One day, as his mind ran to thoughts of life after work, it occurred to him that he had no relationships with either his wife or his four grown children. He was sitting at his polished mahogany desk making arrangements for his successor as these thoughts, quite unbidden, entered his mind.

With a force that struck deep into rarely touched places within his soul, a single sentence hit him: *I am a lonely man.* Immediately, a second thought hit even harder: *I have no idea what to do about it.* Peter felt shaken. Never before had he felt so mortal, so alone, and so impotent. He was accustomed to taking on big challenges and handling them with a cold courage and efficiency that had earned him respect in the business world.

He left the office early that day, uncharacteristically, and on the way through the outer office felt an urge to say something to his secretary. Without knowing why, he knew that he wanted to "connect" with someone. He simply thanked her for the good work she had done, then awkwardly left. (She later told a friend how different he seemed during that brief interaction—no longer gruff, almost tender.) Without thinking, she smiled at him with a warmth she had never before felt toward him. Peter noticed it.

As he drove home, Peter couldn't get her smile out of his mind. It felt good in parts of his soul that hadn't felt anything for decades. He couldn't explain what was happening, but her smile enticed him with a promise of completeness and rest that his weary soul could not resist.

He admitted the obvious to himself. He was aroused and the excitement was deep. It was the kind of excitement that can be felt only by people aware of their loneliness and longing for relief. The anticipation of more fully enjoying that smile seemed, for Peter, to solve the mystery of life, to bring everything together, to introduce him to levels of satisfaction that would forever end his loneliness. It is more than a cliche when someone in this situation asks, "How can it be wrong when it feels so right?"

Within a few weeks, an affair began that continued for three years, long past his retirement. His wife finally discovered her husband's infidelity and decided—after the initial burst of shock, anger, and betrayal—that she wanted to save the marriage if Peter were willing. Her only requirement of Peter, beyond ending the affair, was that he take a thorough look at his life with the help of a Christian counselor. She was a Christian, and years ago he had made a profession of faith strong enough to get him to church once or twice a month.

The man who eventually walked into my office was fifty-eight years old, distinguished, prosperous, and utterly confused. "I want to build a relationship with my wife," he said, "but I don't know how to do it. And I want to break off everything with my former secretary, but I don't know if I can. I feel so empty, almost scared, and deeply resentful of my wife. But with my girlfriend, everything inside me comes together. It seems crazy, but I sometimes think I'd be willing to give up everything—my kids, reputation, money, everything—just to be with her. But I know it's wrong, and I'm enough of a Christian to be scared to death to walk out on God."

Let me give you just a few glimpses of the story he told, and as you read, ask yourself whether you see him as a victim first, then agent; an agent first, then victim; or truly a victim, but an agent first and last.

PETER'S STORY

Peter described a common sort of family background with the usual variety of highs and lows: the girl who turned him down for senior prom; the victory in the college golf tournament when his dad embraced him for the first time in his life; the moments with his dying mother when he felt a tenderness he'd rarely known; the time his seventh-grade English teacher singled him out in front of the class for submitting the worst essay she had ever read in all her many years of teaching; the first major promotion in business that led to financial prosperity, but failed to make his wife as happy as he thought she should be.

As Peter told his story, two events seemed to provoke more passion than any others. Both, not surprisingly, involved his father.

When he was a junior in high school, Peter began a

lawn-care business to make extra money. After several months of pouring his energies into getting accounts and hiring a crew of buddies to service them, he netted a whopping one-week profit of $200. When he announced his business success at the dinner table, his father beamed and for the first and last time said, "I am really proud of you!"

The second event took place during a weekend visit home from college. Sitting with his father watching a ball game on television, Peter casually mentioned a dating relationship that was slowly dying. For whatever reason, his dad became immediately interested. Encouraged to go on by the unexpected attention, Peter shared his heart. He told of his pursuit of the young lady, and his growing hope that she would one day become his wife. When he made his feelings known to her, she was unpleasantly surprised. The relationship began to crumble from that point. Peter began to cry as he told his dad what had happened.

His father responded with a disgusted look and a harsh comment: "Never play your cards too soon. Or you'll always make a fool out of yourself." Then he turned his attention back to the game.

Reflect on the life of this man. He was designed by God to enjoy the unique pleasures of relating as a man to the people in his world. But deep parts of his world were never touched or affirmed, while other more functional parts were valued. He learned to give himself to no one, not fully, because no one could be reliably trusted to respond as he wanted. The fear that he was alone in the world gripped him. And with passion he determined to look out for himself with whatever resources he thought he had.

After considering this story, ask yourself: Is this man a victim or an agent? Do you see his adultery as the movement of irresistible, deep forces within him? Or do you regard it as sin without excuse and, therefore, to be judged more than understood?

VICTIMS, BUT PURPOSEFUL NOT REACTIVE

Folks holding the first view (victim first, then agent) might be inclined to think that Peter's background taught him terrible lessons about himself that he had been living out for years. His central problem, in their minds, might be a shame covering the tenderness of his manhood that requires him to present himself as a talented, aggressive, but non-relational person. Finding the courage to *nourish his inner child*—a free, passionate human being who longs to love and be loved—and to *set boundaries for himself* within which he could choose to live would define Peter as an agent.

Subscribers to the second position (agent first, then victim) would approach Peter quite differently. Likely, they would insist on the obvious sinfulness of his adultery and hold him responsible for his choices regardless of the shame that had filled his soul for years. Certainly his father had failed him and the pain he felt was legitimate, but nothing that happened to him has any bearing on his responsibility to make the moral choice to repent of his adultery and to love his wife. In significant measure, this view is quite correct. Adultery is sinful and Peter must repent, regardless of other struggles going on within him. But this view leaves out important elements that must be considered.

In my understanding (truly victim, but agents first and last) Peter is a damaged man. The evidence of that damage is his failure to value himself as passionately tender and strongly able to create joy in others through his touch. When moralists take too little account of the deep parts of the human soul, which longs for affirmation but has been injured by disdain, they tend to

encourage a commitment to others that is more disciplined than alive. Husbands do right things but never
release the passion that their wives yearn to receive.
Peter is truly a victim.

He is also responsible for how he has related to his
wife, to his kids, and to his secretary. The core direction
of his life has neither been exposed as wretched nor
shattered by the weight of conviction. Since early days,
his determination to survive in a lonely, damaging
world was built on the assumption that there was no
one good enough to trust with his life. That assumption
needs to be exposed as the fuel for his deepest level of
irresponsibility. The experiences of life strengthened his
natural commitment to look after himself with whatever
resources seemed to be at his disposal.

The specific damage he endured made it seem
reasonable for him to become aggressive—rather than
trusting—and coldly aloof to the tender dimensions
of life. But that decision was no more reasonable than
someone deciding to live without eating because the
threat of food poisoning was real. His inescapable longings for relationship eventually surfaced (as they always
will) and the opportunity to enjoy tenderness without
the demands of full-time relating felt like life itself.
Hence the affair.

Was he responsible for it? Yes, of course. Could
he have avoided it? Yes, but only if he recognized
his choice to preserve his life in a lonely world and
repented of that choice by establishing a pattern of
giving himself to others in ways that were risky. Open-
ing up to his wife about the pain of his childhood;
exploring the ways he had hurt her and failed the children; soliciting feedback from family and friends about
how he affected them; facing his terror of being seen as
a failure and his rage at God for doing so little to equip
him to handle the terror—choices like these would
reflect a good use of his power as an agent and would

reduce the compulsive attraction to the counterfeit joys of adultery by replacing them with a taste of the real joys of manhood.

Neither affirmation of personal value nor exhortation to do right should stand at the center of our efforts to help others. There is a place for both. But the person who understands that we are purposeful beings will expose how we exercise our deepest capacity as agents, how we have been truly damaged by life, and how we respond to the damage by choosing a particular strategy for survival, which makes us vulnerable to a unique set of temptations and disorders. At our core, we are purposeful, not reactive.

CHAPTER FIVE

PEOPLE ARE SELFISH, NOT GIVING

DIGNITY AND DEPRAVITY

A biblical understanding of people requires us to think about two central elements in the human personality. One is exhilarating but easily misused, the other is discouraging and unattractive but, if properly hated, able to give reason for unsurpassed joy. The two elements are *dignity* and *depravity*.

As creatures who bear God's image, we possess a unique dignity. It cannot be erased, and so it will either release its beauty fully in Heaven or forever torment people in hell with its lost opportunity. The dignity of our individuality (the prints on my soul are as unique as those on my fingers) reflects God's creative genius. It reveals something of Him. It defines the self in each of us that, although defaced, can be restored and affirmed through intimate relationship with Christ.

The second element, often obscured by the battle to reclaim our dignity, is unspeakably ugly. To be depraved means so much more than the fact that we sometimes do bad things. Beneath our choices, including the good ones, we are driven by a self-centered energy that disguises itself as healthy (or at least justified) and, therefore, invites others to encourage it. As sinful, fallen men and women with Eden's error stamped deeply within us, we buy into a way of thinking that believes happiness and self-interest are compatible—and more, that the former grows out of the latter.

We are wonderfully unique in our identity, capable of an intimacy with God that makes us feel uniquely special to Him. We are also powerfully deceived by our self-focused approach to life that makes it seem there is no higher pursuit in life than to find ourselves. We are both dignified and depraved.

Both elements need to be understood and well-handled. We must accurately identify and release our dignity so that it becomes a source of joy for God and others. At the same time, we must keep choosing to turn away from our depravity as we become deeply grieved by the damage it does. If we deal with dignity but not depravity, the result will be a short-lived excitement in feeling alive that will end in bitter loneliness. Our Lord warned us that life would slip through our fingers if we grasped it too tightly. If we make the opposite mistake and seek to address depravity without having dignity, we will tend toward a smug legalism, which has as its deepest joy a self-imposed isolation from less-righteous folks.

To avoid either error, we must heighten awareness of both our dignity and depravity, trying to understand them as related elements within us. They are not two parts that can be separately studied from an academic distance. They are rather two words that describe the depths of who we are as whole persons. We are wonderful and terrible at the same time; little gods and little devils whose every motive (at best) is a mixture of virtue and vice. The remnants of original glory remain, but the evidence of corruption is everywhere.

When we misunderstand either element or wrongly

emphasize one above another, we lose any hope of establishing truly intimate relationships. And without meaningful relief from isolation, without at least one good relationship, life is not worth living.

THE EXTREME OF SELF-RIGHTEOUSNESS

Think with me a bit more carefully about the tragedy that follows when we develop an imbalanced appreciation of these two elements. A failure to ponder the mysteries of our dignity as relational beings keeps us safely out of touch with the depths of our longings for love and with the pain of their frustration.

Rather than hurting quite so much, we can think of life as an opportunity to do right things, then carefully list things we can do, and feel good about doing them, whether we create joy in others or not. Denying our yearnings for intimacy and instead focusing on do-able standards of purity give us a self-righteous and sometimes nasty sense of superiority toward people who don't measure up to our standards.

It is more comfortable to think in shallow moral terms than in deeply relational categories, partly because it helps us forget that people, even the most blatantly sinful, hurt badly. Rather than having to enter the overwhelming sorrow of life and looking for a way to survive, moralists take refuge in exhortation and accountability — simple structures for dealing with life that keep everything neat. When we approach life with the energy of moralism, judgment comes out of our hearts more easily, and with more feeling, than compassion. A focus on depravity without a corresponding emphasis on dignity leads to a manageable understanding of sin that turns us into scolding, divisive Pharisees who prefer debate to dialogue, who enjoy defending against error more than reveling in truth, and who value the purity of isolation over the struggles of community.

63

THE EXTREME OF SELF-FULFILLMENT

The other error is no improvement. If we pay more attention to our dignity, concerned more about the loss of self-esteem than the loss of righteousness, then our selfish patterns of relating become a side issue. And, except for a few noisy voices in the Christian world who mistake their strident opinions for prophetic insight, the movement in our culture is in that direction.

We seem far more interested in recovering a good opinion of ourselves than in becoming aware of the unsettling depths of our commitment to do whatever it takes to relieve personal pain. When the imbalance leans that way, we begin to recognize no higher value than our own well-being. We, then, set about to honor that value in an uncooperative world.

The consuming passion with which we pursue our goal of getting our lives together obscures the utter impossibility of that task. We face neither the inevitable loneliness that comes when we chase after a goal no one else is after nor the sheer ugliness of caring about no one as much as we care about ourselves. By admitting neither our final loneliness nor our rank selfishness, we create the illusion of happiness. Often, we manage to feel pretty good for a time. There are pleasures in sin and denial. But the way that promises life eventually leads to death—a lonely, corrupted, resentful existence without meaning or love.

REAL SIN

The Institute of Biblical Counseling (IBC) is aiming at a balanced understanding of both our dignity as image-bearers designed to enjoy relationships and our depravity as fallen people who search for the happiness that only relationships provide in ways that put it out of reach. In the first four chapters, I examined several ingredients that mark us as people of dignity. We're relational, passionate, thoughtful, and purposeful. In this chapter, I look at what it means to be depraved.

Now this is no easy task. Folks committed only to recovering the joy of living often downplay the seriousness of sin. And those who think that nothing matters more than keeping rules (you can recognize them by the pleasure they find in rebuking sin) usually trivialize sin by defining it only in terms of bad things people do. For them, obedience is reduced to behavior change. The real problem with sin goes unrecognized. The subtle, insidious strategies we all have for insulating ourselves from the sorrows of close relationships remain hidden beneath the blanket of outward morality. Neither recovery enthusiasts nor self-righteous moralists deal adequately with sin.

What, then, is an adequate view of sin? What is this problem that we downplay or trivialize? What does the Bible mean when we read that "all have sinned" (Romans 3:23) or "I was sinful at birth" (Psalm 51:5)? How do we allow words that accurately describe depravity like *rebellion, autonomy,* and *wickedness* to roll off our tongues without convicting force? What is the difficulty that in others can look so serious, but in us, especially when life is unfair and hard, seem so understandable?

Handling life's problems well requires that we recognize sin as the root cause of every failure to love, every discouragement that has no remedy, every struggle that destroys our usefulness for good purposes.

Keep in mind as you read this chapter that it is hard to get a really good look at our own sin. It seems so natural; we find ourselves yielding to its energy with spontaneous ease. In the best of homes, we grow up assuming that God is not quite good enough to be fully trusted in every situation. After all, my mother prayed for her father to get well . . . and he died. The evidence seems compelling enough for any jury to find God guilty of not being as good as He claims to be.

In light of that assumption, it seems eminently reasonable and prudent to take over the job of caring for ourselves. Some of us twist self-care into taking care of others (in order to protect ourselves from uncertainty and abandonment). Whatever tactics we choose, looking out for number one flows as easily out of our souls as water from a spring.

Sin, that selfish determination to preserve my own soul at any cost, seems as much a part of who I am as my lungs are a part of my body.

If we are going to understand our sinfulness with meaningful clarity we must begin by acknowledging a simple truth: *Fallenness (the state of being sinful) is not intrinsic to our nature.* God created us relational, passionate, thoughtful, and purposeful. He did not create us selfish. With the serpent's help, we brought that problem on ourselves.

But now that it's here, the problem seems as natural as breathing. And it seems attractive, like a mud puddle might be to an inner-city child who has never seen an ocean and thinks the puddle is as good as it gets. One look at the real thing would, of course, forever change his idea. But without that look, he might splash about in the puddle as if there were no greater delight.

The fall, we must remember, was down. We now live subhuman lives, and recovering our humanness requires that we become less selfish, not that we like ourselves better. Dignity is restored only when depravity is replaced with the energy of love.

But we're like rats scurrying about in a dark sewer, doing our best to decorate our environment with bright colors so that we can live more comfortably, then working hard to convince ourselves that we've created

66

beauty. It is in the very nature of fallenness to decline the invitation to climb out of the sewer (or to move to a beach home) — to enjoy the beauty someone else has created. We trust nothing we cannot control. We think our creative powers must be used to overcome our dependence on someone else (including God, because we think even He can't be fully trusted), so we value only those solutions that we design. Humility is not our strong suit.

REAL CONVICTION

It is hard, I repeat, to get a good look at our own sin. Most of what we call conviction is little more than guilty pressure to clean up our lives. But often that is not conviction at all. True conviction involves the shameful awareness that we are wrong and *deserve* judgment, rather than the more comfortable sense of feeling caught and *fearing* judgment.

We can know our awareness of sin is shallow when it provokes only an irritated obligation to do better. A cry for mercy and a longing to be righteous indicate that we've been troubled by the right conviction.

A good look at sin generates an awareness of terror more than a sense of pressure, or even guilt. It brings us close to the realization that we are desperately working to preserve ourselves against the forces of an uncaring world. When we begin to see those efforts as something to abandon rather than develop, we feel the terror. Something grips us by the throat; we struggle to breathe and, in the process, become aware of a deep rage: "Why is life this way? Why is it so hard? Why isn't God doing more to help?"

Facing the terror shatters the illusion that we have overcome it through our strategies of self-protection. ("If I'm really nice, people will like me and everything will be okay.") With the illusion gone, we are left naked and vulnerable before a God whom we do not trust. If the essential nature of sin is to trust no one unless we can define them well enough to predict and use them, then it can be seen that the root of all sin is a suspicion that God is not good.

I will trust only that individual who convinces me he is good. And the measure of goodness I demand is a visible commitment to securing for me whatever I think I need to assure my happiness.

By that standard, it requires denial, not faith, to call God good. Underpaid jobs, rebellious kids, and unexpected dental bills don't do much to encourage confidence in our heavenly Father's kindness.

But still He tells us He is good, and He expects us to believe Him. He seems to think every failure to trust Him with our lives indicates a moral deficiency within us. To us, the refusal to trust seems reasonable. He hasn't done enough to dispel the terror of life. We had better take on the job.

When we are convicted of sin at the deepest level, we sense a terror closing in on us that leads in one of two directions: either toward a passionate search for a merciful God on whom we can depend or toward an enraged rebellion against Him. Until we are confronted with those two options, we have not wrestled deeply with the real issues of life.

In order to understand the moral disease of self-ishness, in order to realize with convicting passion that self-centeredness has more to do with our lack of joy than either shame or self-hatred, it is necessary to engage in two fundamental struggles:

1. *The struggle with integrity:* facing the terror of existence.
2. *The struggle with doubt:* admitting our rage against God for not being good enough.

The Struggle with Integrity

I recently received a letter from a heartbroken father. His son, a nineteen-year-old, had just tested positive for the HIV virus. When the diagnosis came, he made known his homosexual lifestyle to his parents.

The father told me how, upon hearing the news, his mind was immediately flooded with happy memories of family vacations, Bible memory contests at Sunday school, and washing the car together. But beneath the obvious anguish that seems to make the promise of joy into a cruel mockery, there was an even deeper struggle revealed in his question: "Where have I failed? I did all that I knew to raise a godly child, and now he is both perverted and dying. Is there anything left to trust?"

Listen to what he is saying: There must be a design to life that I have inadequately followed, or perhaps a design that has been incompletely revealed to me. If I did what I should, then God was responsible to do His part, and He didn't. Is there no design? Is nothing predictable? Does God not care?

Fallen people (including redeemed ones) want desperately to believe that there's a certain kind of order to life, a reasonableness and predictability that can give us confidence in expecting desired results from responsible actions. Billiard balls move in a direction determined entirely by the force and angle with which they are hit. Isn't that how all of life works? If we raise our kids properly, they will turn out right. If we tithe faithfully, we'll enjoy financial blessing. If we spend time in His Word, God will clearly reveal to us what we are to do in any situation.

I sometimes wonder if the most difficult reality to face about existence is its chaotic unpredictability. We love to twist the *principles* of Scripture into *promises* so that we can rest in a certain knowledge of what tomorrow will bring. Proverbs 22:6 has received this treatment frequently: "Train a child in the way he should go, and when he is old he will not turn from it." Parents of younger children whose most severe crimes are temper tantrums and back-talk like to think that appropriate discipline, affirming love, and consistent prayer will eventually change a problem child into a responsible adult.

But somehow in our minds, lurking in dark regions that we refuse to illuminate, is the nagging thought that maybe it's not true. Maybe our best efforts at obedient living do not guarantee the results we desire. When we hear that our friend's son has AIDS, we want to find a parental flaw that explains the problem. If we can pinpoint the parents' mistake, then perhaps we can avoid it with our kids.

We quiet our fears by insisting that life be predictable. We need to know that there is something we can do to make circumstances happen as we want. We, therefore, devote more energy to figuring out principles for successful living than learning to rest in the character of God.

But we fail in our quest—inevitably, always, eventually. We fail for one simple reason: God never revealed principles for living that were intended to provide us with guaranteed results. *The principles He reveals are given to guide us in our commitment to reflect His character, not to comfortably organize our lives.* We are intended to trust the goodness of God, not the reliability of principles.

And we are to trust God as we live honestly in this world. Life outside Eden is a mess. Nothing makes enough sense to permit us to find rest in living according to a certain pattern.

But we hate to face that reality. When we lose confidence in an orderliness that equips us to arrange life (job, kids, health) to our specification, all that remains is an inscrutable God. He makes no sense either—at least from our perspective. Lengthy experience with God makes it easier to pretend that life can be organized according to predictable laws than to pretend that God can be similarly organized.

The physical world is relatively predictable. Isn't the relational world of people subject to equally reliable laws? We, therefore, want to figure out how to put our personal and relational worlds together, like a builder studying blueprints, rather than how to pursue God with no higher ambition than to know Him. And yet the Lord said, "This is eternal life: that they may know you, the only true God, and Jesus Christ, whom you have sent" (John 17:3).

A friend wept with me over her frustration with God. Several months ago, a young man she knew well took his life. Shortly afterward, she heard the story of another distraught man, this one not a Christian, who jumped from the fourth floor of a building in an effort to commit suicide. But he landed on something that broke his fall—and he lived, unharmed and in one piece.

Why? Why did one man die and another live? Notice how quickly our minds search for an explanation. "Perhaps God was sparing the believer terrible pain ahead by allowing his suicide to succeed, and maybe the unbeliever was spared to give him the opportunity to hear the gospel." And that may be true.

But we don't know. All we can do is trust God that somehow a good plan continues fully in place. We try to develop trust in God by understanding why things happen and how to organize our lives to rule out severe misfortune. If we understood the whys and hows of life, of course, there would be no need for trust. A predictable world would require nothing other than conformity to its principles.

But life is not predictable. And every effort to think it is reflects our demand that life make enough sense for us to manage it. As long as we can hang on to the illusion that life is a reasonable affair, we will not have to face how little confidence we have in God.

The struggle with integrity revolves around our demand that we never feel the terror of living in an unfair, irrational, and chaotic world with no one to trust but God. We will not understand our arrogant inclination to call Him bad until we face the terror of life as it really is. Only then will our true attitude toward God be realized. And only then will we see how selfishly determined we are to believe that life is orderly to a degree that permits us to manage it.

The Struggle with Unbelief
The more we realize there is no pattern to life that guarantees results when we live a certain way, the more we will be confronted with our attitude toward God. We demand that such a pattern exists in order to preserve us from having to face the random terrors of life. And we are determined to avoid that terror because we are not deeply persuaded that God is good enough to fully trust.

If we are interested in handling life's problem by getting down to the root of things, we must understand a long neglected truth: Nothing has ever changed the heart of man, and nothing ever will—other than,

- The refusal to trust God as entirely good (Adam introduced this into human nature and passed it on to every human child ever born); and

- The revelation of God's grace that exposes the extent of His goodness (this revelation could not be given apart from man's sin and Christ's sacrifice and resurrection).

Ever since Adam concluded that God could not be trusted with the unanticipated problem of a disobedient wife, his descendants (both men and women), have agreed that certain difficulties in life go beyond God's ability or willingness to handle. This suspicion that God is not worthy of absolute trust lies at the root of all that it means to be depraved. Until that suspicion is exposed, until our unbelieving attitude toward God is identified as the central dynamic behind every unloving reaction to life, we will handle our problems superficially at best, creating the illusion, never the reality, of peace.

Building self-esteem, releasing the shame that binds us, committing ourselves to obedience, understanding the intricate relationship between past abuse and current struggles, repenting of sins against others, getting in touch with our feelings, acknowledging our deepest longings—nothing will generate godliness in the midst of our problems until we acknowledge our struggle to believe God is completely good and our refusal to trust Him enough to serve Him in the middle of pain.

When we approach God with the bowed head of the publican, crying for mercy because we see how deeply we've offended Him by calling Him bad, then along with forgiveness comes the beginning of an awareness that will eventually overflow within our hearts: He isn't angry! He's actually smiling! There's no look of disdain on His face! His arms are open wide! I spit on Him and He wants to hug me! I've never seen anything like it!

God is compellingly attractive—when He's fully revealed. Theologians call it irresistible grace. Our hearts have been changed from innocent to arrogant because of our suspicion that God isn't good. And they change from arrogant to grateful (and progressively trusting) when we see that the rest of the story had not been told. He's better than anything our experience has led us to expect. No one is good, not like Him. Therefore, only He is worthy of worship.

When bad things happen — when sons commit suicide, when unmarried daughters get pregnant, when jobs are lost, when accidents snuff out a life — our struggle is with belief. Is He really good? Does He mean to harm us or to prosper us? Does He know how deeply we hurt and how much we long for relief? Is He aware that our confusion threatens to destroy any remaining faith under the weight of cynicism and despair?

Satan's preoccupying goal is to keep the revelation of God through Christ under wraps. He toils to persuade us that there is no adequate reason to believe God is good. He points to the injustice and heartaches of life as evidence that God is not worthy of trust. Satan strives to deceive us, as he deceived Eve, into thinking God is holding out on us, that He who gave His own Son would withhold something good from us.

And to achieve his diabolical purpose, Satan has one central strategy: encouraging us to focus on everything but the one thing that provides God the platform to fully reveal His grace — our sin. Satan encourages us to:

- Notice another's sin more than our own.

- Define sin as less heinous than it really is; perhaps regarding it as understandable, in some cases even desirable.

- Explain sin as a legitimate reaction to life's disappointments and, therefore, worthy more of compassion than judgment.

- Think of self-hatred and shame as a more serious problem than sin.

- Treat sin as something merely naughty, like a childish prank.

- Evaluate sin as a merely regrettable path to legitimate relief from pressure and pain — a path made necessary by whomever designed the world.

- Blame our problems on something correctable by improved education or a more civilized society or opportunities for fuller self-development and self-expression.

When Satan is successful in any of these clever methods, the stunning reality of God's gracious character is obscured, undervalued, taken for granted — and its power to change us is blocked. As long as we focus on life's trials and disappointments, feeling our pain more deeply than we feel the pain we cause God, we will struggle to believe in His goodness! Our faith will be sufficient to handle the good times and we will say, "Isn't God good! I just got a raise." But when bad times come, the rage within us against a heavenly Father who treats His children so poorly will spoil faith, eliminate worship, mock the virtue of servanthood, and rob us of joy.

Our culture has lost its sense of sin. We see God as more cuddly than holy (until He fails to bless us) and ourselves as more intriguing and damaged than unworthy of blessing. Without a shattering grasp of personal sin — our sin of calling Him bad — there will be no compelling vision of grace! And without a vision of grace, there will be no meaningful movement toward trusting Him enough to release us to care about someone other than ourselves. Only the absolutely unique kindness of God, revealed most fully when He died for people who hated Him, will draw selfish people toward genuine love.

The only problem that God promises to do anything about — in this life — is our selfishness. He provides no guarantee of financial prosperity, good health, or satisfying reactions from people. God seems obsessed with developing in us a selflessness rooted in a recklessly joyful confidence in Him as the only route to abundant living. And He refuses to budge from that obsession even in the face of our insistence that something more than the power to love another is required for joy.

We know what we need to be happy. Why doesn't He respond to our needs? How can we call Him good when He puts a basket of fruit under the Christmas tree when we asked for a bike? God's position seems to be that we will not properly value the good things of life until first we value Him. And to value Him means to pant after knowing Him well enough to become radically giving people consumed with the joy of making Him known to others.

So He sets about to make us good in a bad world in preparation for making us happy in a perfect world.

To understand our selfishness and to be substantially restored as the loving, worshiping, giving people He designed us to be, we must face our *struggle with integrity*: Life really is an unpredictable tragedy that provides no rest apart from confidence in God's kind intentions toward us. And we must face our *struggle with unbelief*: God will never be seen as good enough to change us into good people until we see what bad people we are and how kind He is to give us Himself anyway.

CHAPTER SIX

USING THE IBC DISCUSSION GUIDES

೭♦

You're struggling with life, with relationships, with crazy emotions. You want answers! You want help! As you've read the first five chapters of this book, you may have asked yourself, "So what?" If you're planning to use one of the discussion guides in this series from the Institute of Biblical Counseling, what difference will it make that people are relational, passionate, thoughtful, purposeful, and naturally self-oriented?

COMMUNITY

First of all, we've designed these as *discussion* guides rather than self-study booklets because the best place for relational people to sort out their problems with relationships is in a group of fellow strugglers. You can certainly benefit from reading or working through one of the guides on your own, but you'll find it enormously helpful to talk about your responses with at least one other person.

Other group members see perspectives on an issue that we would never think of. We may not know how we come across to others, but group members can tell us, if we're open to hearing their feedback. It feels wonderful to encourage someone else in a struggle we've been through or to have them identify with what we are feeling. To have someone listen to and care about our pain is a taste of Heaven.

That's what we like about groups. Knowing what we *don't* like, though, can be just as helpful. Remember that what all of us most long for is to give and receive deep parts of the soul in relationships. And what we most fear is that no one is either offering what we want nor interested in what we have to give. From this terror stems our determination never to feel the horror of isolation. That determination moves us to distance ourselves from people and hide our needy and vulnerable parts.

The very act of discussing these issues in a group begins to reverse that process. In order to answer the questions in these discussion guides, we'll have to begin revealing our neediness, offering our hearts, and receiving kindness and neediness from others. In doing so, we risk the terrors of being misunderstood, ridiculed, or simply ignored. In fact, it's virtually guaranteed that a group of self-centered people will eventually hurt us. When that happens, we'll have the option of facing the pain and continuing to offer ourselves or of retreating in fury. Only God gives adequate reason to keep doing the former; getting involved in real community paints us into a corner in which our only hope is God.

So if the idea of using one of these guides in a group seems equivalent to eating glass, give your reasoning a second look. In order to make lasting progress in these issues, you'll need at some point to begin talking with a few others about them.

Facing damage and guilt will hurt, and risking in relationships will terrify. If you hope for lasting change in yourself, you'll have to be motivated more by a desire to know God and to live God's way than by wanting to feel better.

TRULY VICTIMS

The titles of many of these discussion guides refer to problems with which we all struggle. But because we're relational rather than mechanical, we can't approach anger, guilt, or loneliness as problems to be fixed. Instead, we have to begin to discover our longings to give what no one wants and to receive what no one is offering. The goal of these guides is to help you maneuver through your defensive layers of denial into frustrated longings, damage, and harmful responses hidden in your heart.

As you work through any of these guides, you'll spend substantial time exploring painful memories and feelings. Make it your aim to uncover your *relational style*, which is usually geared toward protecting yourself against re-experiencing that pain.

When asked to reflect on your past and present hurts, you may find yourself minimizing the hurt with statements like, "It wasn't that bad. Many people have it worse." Or, "God has dealt with that. It's all covered by His forgiveness." Again, you may find yourself talking about terrible pain as though you were reporting the weather, as though it happened long ago to someone you don't care much about. You may want to make excuses for everybody else so that all the fault is yours, or you may want to blame everybody except yourself.

Try to be aware when you're inclined to minimize, distance yourself, excuse, or blame. At those times, let yourself feel the pain squarely and face how much you long for someone to comfort you. If you're tempted to shut out God or other group members, choose to let them in. Can you welcome comfort without demanding it?

At the same time, you'll find that the others in your group are also truly victims — who long for comfort but may often reject or demand it. You'll need to take their damage seriously, hearing their pain with compassion and not letting them get away with minimizing it.

Your group is like a living organism — "If one part suffers, every part suffers with it; if one part is honored, every part rejoices with it" (1 Corinthians 12:26). One of your jobs in the group is to "mourn with those who mourn" (Romans 12:15). It's sometimes hard to hear another's story because it touches memories and feelings in us that we'd prefer to forget. Be aware when you feel like leaving the room or changing the subject; you may find a clue to something you need to see in yourself.

On the other hand, some people are spiritual exhibitionists. They delight in detailing their sufferings in order to obtain attention and sympathy. Don't let yourself or other participants get away with this. You or your group leader may have to take an exhibitionist aside to discuss how he or she is affecting the group.

Likewise, while comforting others is often appropriate, we must resist the temptation to rescue people from their pain. Each person must be allowed to feel the full pain of his hurt and the consequences of his choices. Behind the compulsion to mother (or father) everyone who weeps lies a refusal to tolerate pain and a determination to control the situation.

AGENTS FIRST AND LAST

You'll spend considerable time in your group exploring the damage you've each suffered. But it will be important not to stop there. The guides give equal or greater weight to examining how you've chosen to sidestep God and protect yourself from others. Self-hatred will surface as a serious problem, but you'll encounter self-centeredness as an even greater problem. Hatred of God will emerge as the paramount problem.

You'll be looking for the ways you answer these three questions from chapter 3:

- What can people do to either damage me or make me feel good?

- What is there about me that people are likely to criticize or respect?

- What do I have that people sometimes want?

The style of relating that you've chosen flows from your answers to these three questions. Therefore, as you hear one another's stories, listen not just for damage but also for signs of answers to these questions. Recall the questions we asked about Jim: How was he disappointed? What was it about him that disappointed others? What did he think he could offer that might relieve his sense of aloneness?

Your group can help you see aspects of the way you relate that aren't apparent to you. To take advantage of this help, though, you'll need to adopt a humble frame of mind, not blaming others or justifying yourself. You'll need to be willing to hear what others have to say.

At the same time, your group must become a safe place for participants to give and receive feedback. If you have members who delight in confronting others without facing their own critical hearts, you or your leader will need to work with those people. If you sense that someone is confronting in order to gain authority, revenge, artificial intimacy, or something else unloving, you should intercept the criticism, even if it is accurate. We win the right to confront by demonstrating our willingness to face our own wrongdoings and to struggle alongside the person being confronted.

INVOLVEMENT WITH GOD

Because we are more passionate than reasonable, pressure will not ultimately change any of us for the good. Therefore, you should avoid not only selfish confrontation but also every form of subtle pressure: innuendo, advice, and preaching during prayer. If prayers like, "God, please teach Mary that . . ." go unchallenged, participants will learn (with good reason) to shut out anything another group member prays for them. Group prayer can be enormously helpful if it flows from hearts committed to each other's good, but it can be lifeless if it is a mere formality, or positively harmful if it arises from arrogance.

We've seen that escape from the terror of isolation can come to us only from someone who guarantees a perfect relationship and offers a taste of it now. That someone can only be God. And for passionate people, that relationship cannot be merely dutiful. It must be passionate. No discussion group can make that happen, but it can provide an environment that either encourages or snuffs passionate involvement with God. Your group should be a safe (but disturbing) place for participants to question and wrestle with God.

Also, each session in the guides ends with a suggestion for directing prayer on the topic at hand. It will be up to you to make that prayer time more than an exercise. Any member can set an example of honest, passionate prayer.

However, some in your group may panic at the idea of praying aloud in front of others, especially about their deepest fears and pains. At your first meeting you should come to some agreement about how you'll handle prayer together.

We've also observed the damage done when people handle God and the Bible in ways that make them boring. Chances are high that the members of your group have adapted their faith in one or both of the ways we've mentioned: killing their passion with orthodoxy and respectability, or injecting their religion with whatever makes them feel alive. You may want to watch for these traits in yourself and others, so that you can come to an understanding of true living faith.

These guides handle the Bible differently than you may be accustomed to. It's common for Christian writers to sprinkle their arguments with scripture references proving their case. Bible study guides often ask you to look up a great many short excerpts from throughout the Scripture. We've tried to avoid these practices, which Bible scholars call "proof-texting." Instead, we've based our arguments on themes throughout the whole of Scripture: the nature of human beings, sin, repentance, and so on. When we ask you to examine a short passage from the Bible, you'll be encouraged to develop a *relational focus*: How does the passage apply to current issues in your relationships?

TAKE THE RISK

Much more could be said about conducting discussion groups, especially on topics as vital (and volatile) as these. If you're leading a group for the first time, you might want to read one of the following: Gerald Corey, et al., *Group Techniques*, second edition (Brooks Cole, 1992); or Neal F. McBride, *How to Lead Small Groups* (NavPress, 1990). But don't let the complexities of group interactions scare you. The risks of entering a group are the same risks we face every day in relationships—the risks these guides are designed to help you face and flourish in.

EPILOGUE

੨੩

In this booklet, we have studied five elements that go into our make-up as people. We are:

- Relational people who long to love and be loved.

- Passionate people who move through life with a compelling energy.

- Thoughtful people who reach conclusions about God, ourselves, and others that guide us as we live.

- Purposeful people who decide what direction to take as we try to handle life.

- Selfish people who are determined to find some way to survive in a terrifying world without ever trusting God.

As you struggle with problems in your life, as you study the discussion guides in this series, let me encourage you to take a close look at who you really are. Realize how God made you. Face what's wrong within yourself that God wants to forgive and change.

Admit what is in you that God wants to develop and release but that you're terrified to offer to anyone.

Don't settle for shallow solutions. Pretending to be happy when you're not, refusing to face how lonely or scared you are, trying hard to do all the right things in the hope that God will give you what you want, exploring your soul to understand yourself rather than to find God—none of these directions leads to joy.

Take the long, winding road through agonizing questions, unbearable suffering, and shattering self-awareness as it creates within you an earnest desire to know God.

For when you come to Him, slowly learning to trust Him as the good God He claims to be and believing that He does reward those who diligently seek Him with a clearer glimpse of His beauty, then something wonderful begins to happen. Those problems that result from a lack of faith fade away, and those that continue as an inevitable part of life in a fallen world become opportunities to know Him better and to reflect to others your confidence in His goodness.

The struggle is real and, at times, excruciating. As you walk this unexpectedly long path, the next low seems lower than the last one. You sometimes wonder if you're making any progress at all. You think no one could want you as you are. The pressure to handle your problems better can be intense, even from those who love you. You will have moments when perspective is entirely lost: God seems remote and indifferent; family and friends seem impatient, critical, and disgusted.

But still you continue. You know God is good. There is hope. You fail this time, but then you find the power to resist temptation. You do something kind. You trust. You obey. And then you become aware of something stirring inside you. You listen to your heart. As the Apostle Paul did in Philippians 3:10, you will hear yourself saying (and it will surprise you), "I want nothing more than to know Christ, to know His resurrecting power that frees me to act more like Him in all my relationships, and to fellowship in His suffering so that I can even more clearly reveal how good He is to a world that is still suspicious."